NevaEva

Presents:

How to turn a boyfriend into a HUSBAND.

Written by author Isaiah Donaldson Jr.

This book was written for the purpose of educating all women, of all races, ethnic groups, and backgrounds.

I would like to dedicate the very first copy of this book to my beautiful daughter Isabella.

She is only a child but when she is old enough to understand this book I want her to master it.

Introduction

Hello to all of my beautiful, confident, and intelligent female companions.

This book was written for all of you that are ready to hear that big question.

"Will you marry me?"

There are so many beautiful women just like you that go into relationships not knowing how to reach that goal of peace, love, and matrimony.

Unconsciously, most people behave according to how they were taught.

Also by the behaviors they see and hear.

This is the main reason why most women fall short of obtaining this happiness when they want or deserve it.

Many women get married in their lifetime, but in return many women get divorced. A divorce is not something that can be predicted all the time and sometimes can't even be avoided.

No matter what, marriage is something great that should be planned and truly understood.

Marriage is a beautiful experience in life that brings two individuals together in which they agree to love, teach, bond, and grow with one another. Through all obstacles of life. A lifetime partnership.

The reason that so many women go through life without a husband is because they lack the knowledge and understanding of how to turn a boyfriend into a husband.

Now this lack of knowledge doesn't just go for the angry women that everyone says can't keep a man.

Let's just be real.

It's a lot of nice women in the world that don't know how to seal the deal either.
Sadly this is common in a society like America. Why? Simply because peace, love, happiness, and marriage are subjects that are not spoken about in school.

There is no daily curriculum on how to make a person feel special! Not even a class on partnership!

What are the chances of a pretty little girl growing up in life without being taught how to treat her spouse and one day out of thin air she learns it?

The only way to learn anything in life is to be taught or to learn from experience.

The worst thing about learning lessons through experience is that a person might learn bad habits and not truly understand that they're bad.   Most little girls have bad encounters with boys growing up.

Not every experience is bad, but because little boys aren't necessarily taught the same fundamental skills of communication with the opposite sex they tend to move off of their natural instincts.

With that thought in mind you think about this.

What does a boy with no true knowledge of companionship + a girl with no true knowledge on companionship equal?

Happiness?

OF COURSE NOT!

Loyalty?

Heck no!

But a divorce in months or years if you ask me.

So with that being said, in order for a woman to develop the understanding of turning a boyfriend into a husband she herself has to be re-educated.

Before I keep going. I know it's a few women reading this going crazy because she doesn't understand what I mean by turning a boyfriend into a husband.

So before you or they wreck that pretty little brain trying to read between the lines, let me explain briefly what I mean.

The ability to turn a boyfriend into a husband is the way of manipulating a man's mind into seeing the full potential in a female companion.

If a man doesn't understand that there is no other relationship that can benefit him like yours, he will not see the significance in making you his wife.

Even if his first intention wasn't to marry you. If he sees that you're the best woman for him and there's no other woman that can help him become a better man.

He has no choice, but to do whatever he has to do to keep you.

The subject here is learning your man.

The objective is to make him the best he can be.

Why?

"Why would I want to make a man better" some of you might be thinking.

Or, "why am I trying to help a man be better, I shouldn't have to do that because I'm not his mother."

Now ladies if you find yourself thinking things like that, then you really need this book because that was not a joke.

Without this knowledge you might be in trouble. The first thing that you have to learn as a woman is that a man will be a man without you.

But just like anybody else, your man will behave differently when put in different environments.

It's called adapting.

Men, just like women, respond differently when spoken to differently. Everyone has the potential to do better, but when put in different environments, everyone does things differently.

Your goal for a relationship should be to reach the fullest potential of happiness and success as partners that you can reach.

For example, Michelle Obama's husband Barack Obama. He was voted to be the first African-American president of the United States of America.

Barack and Michelle were married years before he attempted to be the president. Who knows what obstacles were in his way possibly hindering him from running in such a big political race.

I mean that is such a giant leap in life, that you have to stay focused and have positive focused people around.

Sometimes the pressure could have gotten to Barack.
Without a great support system how could he overcome adversity.

His wife Michelle just like any other marriage is the closest person he has to him. Which means she had to be there through the good, the bad , the ups, and downs.

Imagine what part she played in his success. Trust me she played a major part. There were certain situations in their life where she did something, anything.

If his wife was someone else, she probably wouldn't have done it.

If Barack had a different wife she probably wouldn't have helped him become president.

It probably was Michelle that told him for the first time in his life that he could do it.

Basically what I'm saying is that the outcome of a man can be altered depending on what type of relationship he is in.

One woman could influence a man to become a present and another woman could influence him to become a drug dealer.

So for all of the women reading this, I truly need for you to take the time to read this book.

This could be the difference in your marriage.

You could marry a man who has the potential and possibilities to become a Barack Obama or a McDonald's cashier.

Each chapter was written and analyzed only to teach all women one thing: " how to turn a boyfriend into a husband."

Chapter1:

Understanding Marriage (psychologically)

Now ladies, it's time to be upfront and real with you.

Okay!

I'm going to be as real as I can be in the most honest, street, political way as possible.

So all of the different types of readers can understand and value my words.

Follow me here.

The first step to turning a boyfriend into a husband is understanding what a husband is.

No, Shaniqua, it is not your baby daddy.

A husband is an equal companion in life. A best friend. But all in all a secondary father to his wife.

Now don't throw my book away after you read that talking about, "oh no, ain't no boyfriend going to think he is my father."

Please just try to understand me clearly.

Secondary father!

A husband is the man responsible for a woman after he swears in front of a pastor, their families, and God.

He swears that he will take care of her.

Marriage is a contract by the law in which it makes two people responsible for one another.

Think about it.

Marriage has been around for thousands of years.

Not to speak about anybody's religious beliefs because we won't, but marriage was even talked about in the Bible.

It's been a part of human life ever since the beginning of civilization. When a female is born, her parents both mom and dad, are her caregivers.

Everything she goes through before adulthood is supposed to be overseen by her parents. They will provide her with knowledge, food, and love.

When the female reaches adulthood and decides to get married and start her own family.
She has what is called a wedding.

A wedding is a ceremony in which her parents (father) gives her to another man.

The man (groom) is given permission by her (the bride's) father to become her provider, teacher, and overseer for the remainder of her life.

This is why the father walks her down the aisle, which symbolizes the long path of life.

He is handing her over to her new caregiver / provider. Now I know that there are some women reading this thinking "what.", but I need for you to visualize the marriage process from start to finish so that you can understand what marriage truly is psychologically.

Marriage is not something that should be taken lightly.

In order to achieve the goal of peace, love, and matrimony. You have to truly understand it.

Now let's break it down. Before most people become adults they live with their parents. A lot of people grow up in single-parent homes or homes with a stepparent. No matter what the situation is, it still takes two parents to start a family.

Two parents!

Once a child is born, the parents are held to a certain standard by the universe.

Even the law.

As a parent it is your job to make sure you do the best to your knowledge to raise your children.

No matter how old a child is 1, 2, 15, or even 22 years old.

As a parent it is your responsibility to show that child the way of life.

If a 3 years old gets in trouble at daycare.

Who will get the bad report?

The parents. Right?

Okay.

So now, further on in life when that same child becomes an adult and gets married. They have both male and female sworn before God to become each other's new overseer in life.

They will now be held accountable for each other's actions.

If a married woman gets into a car accident.

Who will be the first to get the report?

Is it her mom, her father, or her husband?

Of course, her husband!

When a male and female become married their credit scores even become jointed.

Which means the credit bureau considers them now one entity.

A male and female become each other's secondary parent when they get married.

End of discussion!

No I'm not saying call your husband daddy, even though a lot of women do, but I am saying respect him as a father-like figure.

In return he should respect you as a mother-like figure.

After all he is the man that you love, trust, honor, protect, and provide for. It's also up to you to give him the respect he deserves.

The purpose of marriage should not be to stop yourself from being bored all the time.

Ladies, if you are just bored, get a hobby.

If you want a lifetime partner and companion then you get married. There are a lot of women that get married who are not willing to respect their husband as if he was their father.

These are the women that end up getting a divorce.

Not to sound harsh, but Shaniqua can't keep a man because she doesn't know how to treat a man!

Once again this goes back to me saying there are no daily curriculum on how to make a person feel special!

Not even a class on partnership! Because school doesn't teach about marriage, a lot of people go without the proper knowledge on that subject.

The truth of the matter is. Without a first father figure in a woman's life to show her how to respond to a man, she's not guaranteed to know how to respond to a secondary father.

A wife is a man's trophy. But the only trophy that is put on a higher shelf than hers, is his mother.

Why? Because his mother is his first female companion.

She was the one that provided for him when he wasn't able to provide for himself.

Before he was your soon to be husband, he was her very small boyfriend.

Now pause for a second so we can get a few things clear.

Boyfriend and girlfriend are words that are used in the English language to identify a certain gender counterpart.

The true word for this is simply companion.

All right!

Okay!

Now back to the facts at hand.

A mother is a boy's first female lover / companion. She has a lot to do with the characteristics and behaviors that he develops growing up.

Because of this, most boys tend to attract or become attracted to women that are similar to their mom.

Most of the time this attraction is not on purpose but unconscious..

Why?

This is a common question.

Why do men choose women that remind them of their mom?

Simply because she is the first woman that he has ever known. He knows how to behave around her and respond to her.

This makes a girlfriend easier to understand. You only know what you know because of what you've seen and what you were taught.

Now because you as a woman weren't taught to be like his mom, you don't truly know if you're compatible with him when you first meet him.

This is the main reason why a lot of people don't get married. It's hard to overcome the subconscious mind. I mean how can you override the psychological state of a person's mind, when you don't even know what it is.

Now let me educate you a little more ladies because by no means do I want to confuse anyone, all right. In Webster's dictionary the word subconscious is defined as existing in the mind without entering conscious awareness / mental activities below the threshold of consciousness.

Now study that word ladies because it is a keyword that I'm going to need for you to remember. Ok.

So basically the subconscious is teachings that a person learns without knowing.

The unconscious mind is what operates beyond the control of the person.

In which ultimately turns into the person behaving a certain type of way without trying and most times even without knowing.

LOL.

I just got a feeling that one of you is closing this book right now because she could not comprehend what I'm saying.

Ladies if you are still reading this I need for you to get a pen and underline subconscious, please!

Not saying that like it's a word or something, but because it's a keyword that plays a big part in understanding life. A boy learns from teachings and experiences of life.

All experiences don't bring forth good lessons, but they all embed teachings in the mind.

This is what is meant by the subconscious.

When the boy deals with his mom for most of his life he gains the knowledge of her and only her.

He knows what she likes, doesn't like, and he knows how to behave around her. When he gets older he tends to treat women according to how he treated his mom.

Some guys have better experiences with their moms than others. But no matter what, every boy has thoughts and lessons learned from experiences with their mom.

That will play a part in his success and his relationships.

So understand the same way those thoughts and lessons learned can play a part in his successful relationships.

It can also play a part in his unsuccessful relationships.

Let's just keep it real ladies.

All moms do something to their sons that they don't like. It could be something small like refusing to give him candy before dinner or something big like verbally abusing him.

Now depending on what that something is, he is going to already be subconsciously programmed not to like it .

Example: Jerome's mom used to yell at him not cleaning up behind himself. She yelled so much that Jerome was scared of her. He was so scared that he taught himself how to hide his unclean nature, so that he wouldn't get yelled at.

He didn't like cleaning so he didn't truly learn to clean, but he learned to act like he was cleaning to avoid getting yelled at. Now later in life when Jerome is an adult, here comes his new girlfriend Shaniqua. He is an adult now so he consciously feels free of childhood guilt. So he starts to be who he is in his natural form, little dirty Jerome.

Why not though? He is not a scared little kid anymore. He is a grown working man and here comes Shaniqua yelling at him about being unclean.

Oh man she doesn't even know that Jerome's mother used to say those same exact words.

"Jerome, you are living like an animal, you need to clean up."

Why did she say that? She just brought back childhood fears from when his mom used to yell at him. But the only difference is Jerome is grown now and doesn't view Shaniqua as a secondary mom.

Trust me he isn't putting up with that! Now look at Jerome yelling back at her. " Don't tell me what to do, you ain't my mama."

LOL. Believe me, Jerome has been holding back a lot of anger from his childhood. He has been waiting to snap on somebody. Why? Simply because he bottled up those emotions as a kid out of respect for his first love/mom.

Which one day was bound to come out on someone and look at who it was. Poor little Shaniqua. Sorry Shaniqua, you didn't even know that anger existed.

Neither did Jerome. This is how the unconscious and subconscious mind work. Now for all of you out there, I need for you to understand why this is important.

This is the main thing you need to focus on when trying to turn a boyfriend into a husband. You will need this tool because you are trying to fix the bad stigma in your man's mind that he has lived with and accepted from his mom.

Of course some women are out there saying that sounds like a lot, but so does cooking a full meal.

Until you learn how to view marriage, you will not know how to achieve it. Anyone can get married after dating a hundred people, but how many women can say that they know how to turn a boyfriend into a husband.

This should be the goal, not dating several men for years. Giving each individual man years of your life only to say that they really wasted your time has to suck.

No longer shall you waste your time on the dating scene. For now on after reading this book you should understand the key fundamentals of marriage.

You should look at your chosen counterpart/ companion as your secondary father figure. In return you are his new mother figure.

He should respect you as if you are his mother. You have to get into his mind to find out who he is mentally.

How he thinks plays a major part in how he acts. Now even though he has already learned lessons growing up from his mom, he can still be taught and adjust to another woman's behavior.

So when moving forward don't think of this process as if you are putting in too much work for a man.

Understand that you are training a man subconsciously how he should respond to you and treat you. If he'll be a part of your life, he needs to know how to treat you.

He did not learn about your feelings and emotions in school. He doesn't know what makes you mad. He just knows about women from what was previously taught to him. Now as his girlfriend, you take on the responsibility of his new teacher.

You have to teach him about you in order for him to know about you! Not knowing about the counter spouse is the main reason America has so many divorces every single year.

Mainly because once again I have to mention the fact that there is no daily curriculum on how to make a person feel special! Not even a class on partnership.

When a woman attempts this process of turning a boyfriend into a husband, she has to understand that all men can be turned into a husband.

Just like all women can be loved, all men can be loved as well. The only difference in my theory is understanding that all people cannot be joined together as companions.

The hardest part about turning a boyfriend into a husband is choosing the right boyfriend.Most people choose a spouse because of a physical attraction to one another.

Less people focus on mental attraction. But in order to consider someone as a friend or companion it has to be a mental connection between people.

Of course when two people lock eyes for the first time in the mall, club, classroom, gas station, or anywhere for that matter. The physical form is the only thing noticeable.

But once a person speaks, you can hear what kind of mentality they have.

Now of course growing up in a society like America where fashion is glorified. Of course, it's easy to focus on the outer appearance of someone.

But in order to have a relationship that is successful, two people have to be somewhat on the same mental capacity level. This is what makes two people compatible.

Love, peace, happiness, and matrimony are psychological things more than anything. You know what ladies get your pen! No I'm serious, get your pen ladies and underline psychological please.

Now remember this process is not truly focused on anyone more than it is focused on you! I want you to take control of your life so that when you find yourself saying "I'm ready for marriage" you can accomplish that goal.

I have a saying / slogan which is "to reach the goal of empowerment, we have to re-educate ourselves."

Which is true. The only way to achieve happiness in life, is to feel within yourself that you are in control of life. Self-empowerment is the goal of life!

So with that being said ladies keep these two key words in mind as you move forward to chapter 2. Matter of fact keep those two words in mind for life! Subconscious and psychological.

Chapter 2:

Understanding the spouse (psychologically)

Hello beautiful. How are you? Can I ask you a question? Do you know yourself?

Really, that's not me playing around. I told you I'm going to be as real with you as possible. So lets be real.

Do you know yourself? What kind of stuff do you enjoy doing? What kind of things do you like to talk about?

All of these things matter when it comes down to reviewing yourself. Before anyone can say that they are ready to love someone, they have to be able to say that they love themselves!

So be real. Do you truly love yourself?

If you do, then you should have no problem following my instructions. Get you a sheet of paper and write down a few things that you enjoy. Like food, TV shows, activities, dates, and anything else that you can think of.

Take your time please, because this will play a big part when it comes to re-educating yourself about companionship.

How was your relationship with your father? How did you two interact? Did he yell or curse at you? How did you feel?

Once again ,this is only to better yourself so when you read this please take it seriously.

Just like how a boy learns how to deal with women from his mom. Women learn how to deal with men from their father or father figure.

Now I need you to think hard. I want you to write down what kind of things you saw your father and mother do together.

If you don't feel like doing this then don't. Just know that you are only missing out on a great teaching method used by great psychologists.

The reason that I'm asking you to do this is because I want you to tap into your subconscious mind.

Did you see your parents fight? Were they happy? Regardless of the answer.

I want you to know that you don't have to base your relationships off of what you saw your parents do. You are beautiful and very smart.

You deserve to be happy.

Every time you look into the mirror you need to smile and remind yourself that you are a queen. All women grow up watching their mother in relationships and subconsciously hold on to what she sees.

Some tell themselves "I want a man to treat me just like my daddy treated my mom."

While others say. "I would never let a man treat me like my father treated my mother."

I just want you to know now that you are grown and that you are in control of your own life. You're also in control of your relationships.

If you want a man to respect you. You first have to respect yourself. If you want a man to respect you, you have to demand respect.

A lot of the time, you have to act the way you want people to view you. For example, If Shaniqua walked into Walmart on the phone cursing and screaming about what she just saw on Love & Hip Hop, how would anyone view her?

They would automatically assume she is "rachet" or is aggressive. But are they wrong for their assumption?

A man is going to respond to a woman according to the way she acts. Now I'm not saying change who you are, but what I am saying is know yourself.

When you truly know who you are, then you will be able to understand what kind of man you are compatible with.

If you are loud, then mostly you will attract a loud man. But the only difference with that is that most people are not compatible with the exact same.

There is a universal law that states that opposites attract. Philosophers like Plato and Aristotle are infamous in history for their scientific theories.

All the way back to the ancient Egyptians the universal law of opposites has been a theory to understand. In this instance the theory basically states that males attract women and vice versa. It also states that negative attracts positive, what goes up must come down, and any other theoretical equation.

So with that in mind, understanding this law will take you far in life. When looking for a companion you need to know that a man that is somewhat different is good.

Why? Because then this gives you new things to learn! So consciously you know what you were taught, but in order to get the full affection of a new companion, you have to go through a new learning stage.

Re-educated. Of course it is easy to act like the old you when your new boyfriend acts like your old one, but the only way to meet your full potential is by entering different environments and adapting.

If your father and your last five boyfriends like to sleep in separate rooms from their spouse, somehow consciously you will accept it. Even if at first you didn't like it, sooner, or later you will start to be okay with it because you will become used to it.

Now one year later if your new spouse wants to sleep in the room with you. It would bring a new feeling to you. It might feel so good to you because psychologically you always wanted it but never got it.

Something so simple could make you so happy because it makes you feel different. Differences are not always a bad thing. Most of the time differences are good, but they never take the time to find out.

People who are uneducated on exploring and changing their environments always miss out on enjoying their lives to the fullest potential.

Now remember before you can love someone else you have to love yourself. I want you to write down on a sheet of paper what makes you happy.

Come on please! I need you to do this before I move on. Write down all the things that all of your ex-boyfriend's have done and said to you that you don't want to happen again.

Think about it for real because this is actually a good exercise. It is called setting morals, values, and standards for yourself.

Before entering a new relationship with a new companion it's great to do this. Why? So that you know what you are willing to deal with.

Remember what I said before, the hardest part about turning a boyfriend into a husband is choosing the right boyfriend.

In order to stop wasting time on guys that have no potential, you have to focus on what you want. Set standards! Once you have your mind made up on what makes you happy, then you are ready to be happy.

Now when you meet a guy you have to be ready to quickly analyze him to see if he is even worthy of being turned into a husband.

What does he like to do?
How does he act when under stress?

You have to learn about him before you can say he is your type. Of course you like cute men. Of course you like strong men. But what else do you like?

Do you like for a man to hold your hand or not? Whatever you like you have to teach him. Nobody can read your mind so if you like to hold hands ask him if he likes to.

Why? Because you want to teach him what you like and how to treat you. Now I'm going to stop right there and say this. Let's be real.

I was talking in circles just to get you ready for the real, but I'm tired of waiting. I'm going to be real with you. So real with you that you're going to love me.

Okay! All right. When you find a guy that you are interested in or attracted to. I want you to understand that you have to tap into his mind.

Love, peace, and happiness is a psychological thing. In order for you to know your spouse you have to know him mentally.

What does he think about? What makes him happy? What makes him mad?

You have to know your man before you can tell yourself that you're ready to marry him. Unless you want five kids from a marriage and then get divorced because he just was different or just wasn't for you.

Before you can say that you know him, you have to know his past. Ask him questions about his life and his relationship with his mom.

Remember she was his first love / companion / teacher. He'll speak to you the same way he speaks to her. Unless you're different.

In this case it may be ok to be different. You want to know what she didn't know.

What made him mad, sad, and happy. Whatever she did to make him mad will always make him mad no matter who is doing it.

I learned this from studying. No, I didn't go to college for a relationship degree but I do study psychology. One thing they do as a method of learning and understanding about a person is psycho- analysis.

Ladies grab that pen with those pretty little fingers again and underline that word for me.

The Webster dictionary defines psycho-analysis as " a method dealing with the psychic disorders by having the patient talk freely about personal experiences and especially about early childhood experiences and dreams.

If you don't believe me just look it up yourself and then you get back to reading.

I'll wait!

Okay, are you ready to re-educate yourself?
Then let's go.

The only way to know a grown man is to know the little boy that he was. Everyone, I repeat everyone who is grown was a kid before.

No one can go back in time to change their childhood, but everyone can review their past in order to take control of the future. Your companion was once a little boy.

That little boy may have been hurt before. Now as a big strong man he may not want the same things to happen to him, so psychologically he will hide it.

You might not understand why he is so angry but before you waste your time dealing with him you need to know who he is mentally.

I'm not saying leave your spouse because of his past. Not at all am I saying that. What I am saying is that you need to learn about his past because it will help in your future.

When a man takes a woman by the hand and can express his true inner feelings, he is opening his heart to her. Now it's about what she does. Her response to his life, thoughts, emotions, and secrets will play a big part in their relationship.

A man, just like any other human being, wants to feel safe. No one wants to confess their true feelings to someone that they don't feel comfortable with.

You want your boyfriend to trust you. The more he trusts you, the more comfortable he will be around you. The only way to express true thoughts is to relax the human mind and body.

Make your spouse feel comfortable and he will pour his heart out to you. The key thing about the psycho-analysis process is to be analyzed.

Pay attention to his feelings. His feelings are the thoughts and emotions that trigger his actions.

He is human, so of course he has emotions. Some women say that the men that seem to not be in touch with their emotional side are most likely hiding something.

Subconsciously when a person is scared in life they tend to bottle up their emotions and not want to talk about it, but that is a key emotion that you and your spouse have to get to the bottom of.

It could be the piece of him that he may be missing and when he overcomes it, he could be the greatest he can be. Let me just ask you this.

If a man reaches his fullest potential mentally because of his girlfriend, who will receive credit for helping him? Think about it! How could another woman compete with the woman that influenced and pushed Barack Obama to become the president of the United States?

There's no competing with Michelle. That's what a wife does. She brings out the best in her husband. Before she notices it, he will gladly let her know.

This is how you turn a boyfriend into a husband. You help him be the best he can be. But before you can help him be the best he can be, you have to know him mentally and emotionally. Ladies before you can marry a man you have to understand your spouse psychologically.

CHAPTER 3:

Becoming a partner

For a lot of people this next topic is not that easy. For many it is complicated, but for a wife it should be very simple. Let's play a game.

The name of the game is success. There are no specific rules to this game, just play it smart. There will be plenty of obstacles in the way, but always remember that the purpose of playing any game is to win.

In order to win this game you have to take advantage of each and every situation. Before this game starts you are to assemble the best team for yourself. Your team is for the sole purpose of achieving the ultimate goal of the game. Success!

Now, before you do anything I want you to ask yourself. Are you on the best team that you can build? Do you feel confident enough in your team that you know there's nothing stopping you from reaching the goal here?

Are there any teammates that make you feel like they can hold you down? If so, you may have a solid team. Your team will play one of the biggest roles in this game because the winner of success will not enjoy success on their own.

Most of the time the winners of success will enjoy their victory with the team that helped them achieve it. There are a lot of people that win this game called success without a team, but no matter what every single winner eventually enjoys it with someone.

Success has many different outcomes. For many it is a financial victory. For others it is an emotional victory. The only common understanding for winners is that it is a psychological one.

The mental accomplishments will be displayed through a person's attributes. See, this is a game in which the outcome of each team can only be determined by each team.

In all reality a person is only as successful as they think. Now don't get me wrong there are different levels of success and most of them can be seen by others.

A person can tell what level of success a person has reached just by spotting them on instagram. Even though pictures don't necessarily prove a person's success.

However, there are plenty of rich people that are not happy. Would you call a millionaire who wants to commit suicide happy or successful? I hope not because that would mean you're in trouble!

Success is a mental and spiritual accomplishment. There are plenty of people who work a nine-to-five every day that feel in their hearts that they are successful and because it is in their heart you can't take that happiness away from them.

People that reach success in their mind, body, and soul are the winners of this game. Now, my goal for writing this book is to ultimately help as many people achieve this psychological happiness as possible, but the only way for me to do that is for you to accept happiness as a possibility.

Now ladies, do you really want to be happy?

Do you really, really want to be happy? If you do, then I want you to know that I believe that you can.

First off, I want you to smile and give yourself props for reading this book this far. No, I'm serious. It's a lot of people that are so stuck in their ways to the point where they would never read this.

Most people who are negatively attached to their belief system will not give anyone the satisfaction of thinking that they can teach them something new, but the truth of the matter is that being taught something new means you had to be taught something old.

We all can be real with ourselves and say that we have not been taught about relationships with the opposite sex or marriage in middle school. So with that being said, be proud of yourself for taking control of your life.

Now let's get back to business.

If you could assemble your team to accomplish success, who would be the star players? This is important, so think about it. What do you need your teammates to do for you to achieve success?

In order to reach this happiness inside yourself, your teammates have to feel secure and because you recruited your own team, you are the coach not a player.

Now before we talk about your players/ teammates I need you to ask yourself one question.

Do you have the leadership skills to help your team win?

After you answer that question you're ready to play.

So let's play.

If you have a boyfriend do you let him be the star of the team or does he sit on the bench while you let him watch? This is a reason a lot of relationships / teams don't make it far.

Why? Because every human being has a purpose. When a person doesn't understand their purpose, they tend to not reach their full potential.

As a coach! It is your job to help all of your players understand their full potential. Now let's be real ladies, no more sugar coating this game.

Your man should be your star player. If he is not he will eventually find another team to be a star player for. As a star player you may be thinking, a star player is the face of the team. Along with the coach that is.

Star players are the most confident people who everyone knows is in control of the game. The coach's job is to make sure the star player is always motivated, relaxed, and always in good situations.

When analyzing your star player you have to see his full potential. I mean he is the one that will ultimately help you achieve success. What are his goals? What does he want to accomplish?

In order for you to help him you have to know these things. It's okay if you're not interested in his individual goals. You don't truly have to be, but what you do have to do is be supportive of them.

No one wants a non-supportive teammate, coach, friend, or family member. Just one non-supportive person in a man's life could hinder him from being great. Of course everyone doesn't see eye-to-eye on every situation, but when two people intend on reaching success together they have to be supportive of one another.

Remember success is a mental achievement. How can two people reach this mental achievement if one is mentally happy and the other is not. When a person has their mind set on being happy, anyone that is not supportive of this state of mine can make them unhappy.

A relationship with someone is more than sex ladies. Sex is not important when it is compared to a psychological happiness. When a man meets a woman he wants to get to know her and the beginning of a relationship is the best time to explore the mind of a person.

Why?

Because this is when people try to impress each other. Simple as that. The first impression between two individuals play a big part in the connection and bond that they can grow together.

People love to talk about themselves. There's nothing more thrilling than hearing someone new tell you how much they value your mental capability.

Think about it. When you meet an attractive man for the first time, what do you talk about? Do you talk about the weather or do you talk about goals?

Most people explain their life in so many words when they first have conversations with others. Speaking from experience, when I first meet people I love telling them what I have going on. Who doesn't?

This is how I get people to understand me better. I, just like most people, don't have the happiest past, but nothing is stopping me from looking towards the future.

When I talk I want people to know my potential. I don't want people to assume anything about me that isn't true, so therefore I will gladly tell them who I am.

If I am not mistaken, all people are like that. Men are nothing more than the male human beings. Female human beings have thoughts, goals, hopes, and dreams just as males. If you want a man to be all he can be for you, then you have to want him to be all he can be for himself!

Motivate him at all times. Ladies don't forget that you want to turn a boyfriend into a husband. What kind of husband is happy if his wife is sad? What kind of wife is happy if her husband is mad?

As a future wife, you want your husband to know you and understand what part you'll play in his success. You want him to value your thoughts. The love of a spouse can be the best thing or the worst.

There are some relationships out there that are toxic. At any given moment they are ready to be blown up. No one wants to be like this, but it's sad to say, there are many people that are living like that everyday.

Well no longer will you put yourself in this type of situation because you are obviously smarter than that. I want you to look at your boyfriend or future boyfriend. Take a good look at who he can be with good guidance and I want you to guide him there!

Make him become who he can be. Not who you want him to be, but the best man that he can be. This is another big thing in many relationships.

Some women don't understand the potential of their men, they just see what they want him to be. So they may push him the wrong way.

Everybody has been influenced but all influences are not good influences. You want your spouse to feel open enough with you to be their true self around you.

You might think that you can help him be better than he wants to be, but at the same time that doesn't mean that it is best for him. What's best for you could be worse for someone else.

Mentally you want your spouse to feel as though his thoughts matter. All in all, it is the ethos that ultimately plays a part in an individual's happiness.

Ladies I need for you to get the pen back out and underline that word. Ethos. I know, I know. I'm starting to be a pain in your side with these words right?

I just want to help you the best way that I can and the only way to do that is to help you see what I see. Webster's dictionary defines ethos as the distinguishing character, sentiment, moral nature, or guiding beliefs of a person, group or institution.

The ethos of a person makes them who they are. Without understanding any individual on a psychological level you can't say you truly understand them.

When attempting to turn your boyfriend into a husband you are trying to share something special with someone. You are basically inviting another soul to bond and grow with yours.

This is why I continue to speak about something more than most people. A lot of people value the physical things that can be seen more than the thoughts of the unconscious person.

Not saying that there's something wrong with liking someone because you're attracted to them, but what I am saying is you should focus on something a lot bigger than that when you are trying to spend the rest of your life with a person.

It is what a person says to you that makes you happy or mad. It is what a person says about a situation that turns a conversation good or bad. So you have to understand that it is more than a cute face that makes a relationship last forever!

The way a person thinks about you will show in their actions and also in the heat of arguments. You don't want to date a guy without knowing him mentally.

Now I mentioned another word just a second ago that I want you to focus on for a second, so get your pen again. Please! This may be the last word that I ask you to underline so take this and meditate on it.

The word is unconscious. Now this word is another key word so be sure to keep in mind when attempting to turn a boyfriend into a husband. Most people have heard this word before. Nothing major.

The truth about this word is that everyone has a different mental state of mind. The Webster dictionary defines unconscious as the part of one's mental life of which one is not ordinarily aware of but which is often a powerful source in influencing behavior.

It will take you time to understand that. Read it three more times just to get a better understanding of what it actually means!

Imagine what you do unconsciously without knowing. For example, who is your favorite music artist? What is their best song that you just love? What is it talking about? It is money, love, drugs, alcohol, or sex?

Whatever it is, when you hear it does it make you dance? What does it make you think about? What kind of mood does it put to it?

That right there!

That thought that you just had when you picture the song playing. That was a conscious thought. It was conscious because you had that thought on purpose. Unconscious behaviors on the other hand happen when you're not trying.

Anything can trigger them like listening to music, watching TV, or hearing someone say a certain thing. No matter what, the unconscious behaviors of a person should be taken seriously.

Remember when I was explaining the situation between Jerome and Shaniqua? Do you remember how he responded to her when she told him how he was unclean?

His response was based upon his subconsciousness, but his unclean behavior was simply an unconscious decision. He didn't even realize that he was being unclean! This is what plays a part and a lot of relationship arguments.

Why? Simply because people don't know each other well enough mentally to correct bad habits. If Shaniqua knew Jerome on a psychological level she would have known not to say that to him.

I'm not saying that she was supposed to walk on eggshells. I'm just saying that she would have understood the fear and pain inside this grown man.

She would know what triggers his anger and she would have thought of a better way to say it. Maybe she wouldn't have said it at all because she would have known that he would get defensive.

Knowing your spouse eventually will be the only way to avoid petty arguments. You have to understand his feelings in order to acknowledge them.

How else do you know how to make him smile? I'm just telling you what I know.

When a man feels comfortable with a woman he will try his hardest to make her feel comfortable. Men love women so much that they would do anything to get their attention.

We all know that but until a woman does the same and shows the same interest for a man, what's the difference between her and all of the rest?

One thing about men is they are easy to get but hard to keep. This goes for most of them. Not because they have short attention spans, but because they are not educated on expressing their emotions. Think about it, what kid goes to school and attends speak your mind class or even how do you feel 101.

Since most men do not experience the proper education on topics about expressing their emotions they tend to just express them through their natural instincts.

The natural instinct of most animal species is to be a protector, tough, and confident. Not sentimental and emotional.

If a man is sentimental around his male friends he is looked at as weak. When male coyotes fight to see who is the alpha male, the losing coyote is exiled from the pack and ashamed.

He is called a coward. Men are the same in certain aspects. All men don't try to hold themselves to a bully tough-guy demeanor but they all do have a certain level of dignity.

When dealing with a man's dignity, this should be something that is not to be taken lightly. A man can respond incorrectly to anyone, including his spouse when he feels that his dignity is on the line.

Self pride is the correct terminology. All people deal with pride, but some men go overboard. Not saying that this is a bad thing ladies, but it is something to consider.

If you really want to turn a boyfriend into a husband you have to pay attention to his behaviors when he is under stress.

When a man is under stress you can see his emotions and actions that are suppressed. This is a natural behavior which can only be described as his rectitude.

The Webster dictionary defines rectitude as moral integrity. If you don't mind, queen could you please underline that word please when dealing with your spouse you have to keep in mind that he is a creature of habit.

No matter what he does or says he doesn't want to make himself feel like he is going against what he stands for. His dignity, morals, and values are all he has.

He lives and responds based upon his beliefs. He could love a person clearly, but when he feels as though that person is not respecting who he is as a man, he will psychologically become on defense mode.

This may be the worst mental behavior for a man in a relationship. Watch him closely and learn him all around the board. If a man becomes psychologically defensive it could ruin the way he views a person.

It's not his short attention span that will make him look at a woman differently, but because of her going against his manhood.

I must remind you ladies that I applaud you for re-educating yourself on this subject of turning a boyfriend into a husband. Just understand that this is not an easy process, but it can be if you are sincerely interested in a man.

When looking at a man you have to remember that before he met you he already held himself to a certain standard. To treat him differently than he wants to be treated will make him analyze you in a different way.

It's okay though. You want him to view you differently so that he can value you on a different scale. Just pay attention to his response. This is what helps decrease petty arguments from turning into relationship enders.

Now I'm just going to keep it real with you ladies. I know it might seem like I'm telling you to ignore your feelings just to keep a man. I'm not. In no way am I expecting you to put anyone's feelings and emotions in front of your own.

I am only saying to value your spouse's emotions as you would want him to value yours. What would you do to your spouse if when he gets emotional, he starts to say things that hurt your feelings?

I'm pretty sure you wouldn't like it. I know you wouldn't and you wouldn't want him to say I didn't know I would hurt your feelings. You should want to know your man inside and out.

Why? Because this is who you intend on spending the rest of your life with. Who wants to be with someone for 5 years and then before actually finding out who they are dealing with.

Oh no not me! I don't want any surprise visits from the angry beast from within. I would rather know if you are an angry person from the start.

Wouldn't you? All right, so this is what I mean all in all about becoming a partner you should know your teammates weakness and power traits. It will play a big role in how well your chemistry is. Remember the ultimate goal for your team should be success!

CHAPTER 4:

Let your king be a king.

Now that we've discussed the easier parts of this process, let's get down to the nitty-gritty.

For a lot of you this may not be hard at all, but for many this could possibly be the hardest chapter for you thus far. With all that being said no matter how hard or easy this is ladies, you are strong enough to do whatever you put your mind to.

When a person wants something bad enough, they can definitely program themself to do it. It's just about how and what you are programming yourself to do. When thinking about turning a boyfriend into a husband you have to be careful with who you pick to do this too.

All combinations aren't the best. Some people bring out the best in people and some bring out the worst. Of course you won't know who's the best for you when you first lay eyes on them, but after you have a few encounters with them, then you can at least give it some thought.

You should be asking yourself "can I see this guy as the leader of my family." Remember when I was speaking in the last chapter about assembling a team. This is almost the same concept but it's different in many ways.

This is somewhat of an inner process. It takes more than a handsome smile or a conscious man to become the leader of the family. It takes a queen to let a king be a king.

Are you a queen? Do you think of yourself as being a diamond in the rough? If you do then I need for you to lift your head up high and say. " I am a queen and I will let my king be a king!"

One more time." I am a queen and I will let my king be a king!" Did you do it? How did that make you feel, ladies?

You should feel like you are in control of your destiny. I want you to feel this way because you really are. You have the power to turn a boyfriend into a husband, but I want you to be real with yourself and truly think about it.

Do you have the power to be submissive to a man? This is a real question for a real woman to think about. Do you have the power to be submissive to a woman?

I don't want to hear " if he's rich." Why does a guy have to be rich for some women to find themselves being submissive? It should not be based on his financial success, it should be because he makes you feel psychologically successful.

Inner happiness comes from within. It's not something that can be bought. Love is a mental thing, not a materialistic object that money can buy at Lenox mall.

To accept love from a man, you have to seek it within yourself. There has to be a level of honesty, loyalty, and respect within yourself. Your husband needs you to commit to his discretion and judgment.

Which means you need to feel confidence within yourself to understand that as his wife he'll need you to follow his lead. Does that make you a follower? Of course not.

It makes you a partner. I'm not saying that if your husband says "let's commit suicide together" then you should do it. By all means do what's best for you in every situation.

I am simply saying that a man's natural instinct is to lead his family. So let him do what he was born to do. Don't take away from his pride, especially if you don't necessarily have to.

If he says this is what we should do, then you need to think about it. Don't automatically go against his wants and thoughts. If he is asking for you to do something which isn't right, then of course you are to reject.

Never degrade yourself to make someone else happy, but for those little things that are not life or death situations you should always give your spouse enough respect by making him feel as though his opinion matters.

You have to always consider how your spouse feels in certain situations that affect your partnership. Why? Because the same way you want to be in control of your life and destiny, so does he.

Everyone wants to feel as though their opinion matters, especially when it's about their life. Now I just want to pause for a second to say one thing.

I was speaking with a few women at a convention in Atlanta, Georgia. It's kind of funny when I think about it. I was in the process of writing the plot for this book and a lady got highly upset with me.

She yelled at me and called me a sexist. I laughed it off, but she was so serious. She asked me "why do you break things down as if the woman has to give up so much and the men don't have to give up anything."

I had to explain something to her and I spoke softly out of respect for the fact that she was angry. I explained to her that when speaking to an individual about their habits, problems, issues, and concerns you have to address only them.

The overall equation cannot be discussed until the individuals involved take both of their actions and acknowledge their role. She didn't really understand why I was saying the things that I was saying.

So if there is anybody reading this book feeling the same way, don't please. I'm only speaking to you this way because the purpose of this is to teach you, but don't worry about them.

When it's time for me to speak to the men, trust me I am definitely going to explain to them what they should do. Their speech will be completely different.

They are not off the hook and they can use their own lessons on how to treat a woman, so don't feel bad. Just understand that the purpose of me breaking down some things to you is because I want you to take control of your life.

I have a daughter and plan on having more. I want them to learn the same things that I am explaining to you. So don't take it hard on yourself.

Now that I've cleared up some things for the silent critics, let's get back to business. If your spouse asked you, "baby girl, how and why should a woman be submissive to her man" or "baby girl hello and why should a woman be submissive to her man?"

When are you able to answer that then you might be capable of trying to be in a long-term relationship? Why? Because for most relationships I repeat most relationships, each spouse is looked at by the other spouse from a certain point of view.

A man should be a man at all times and a woman should be a woman at all times. There is no right way for a man or a woman to be. There are a lot of relationships where the woman dominates her spouse in every way.

Some men don't know how to be the leader of their own home, so the women have to. There are some women that are just better at leading as.

If that is the case in your relationship then do your thing sweet pea. I'm not knocking you. If your man doesn't mind following your lead then carry on.

This is just for those of the majority that do things upon their natural instincts. The natural instinct of a man is to be the leader and protector of his family. The natural instinct of a woman is to nurture and provide for her family.

So when analyzing facts about all, not just some humans, I'm only speaking about what truly works for the majority. When you respect the way someone acts and thinks, they will show you the same respect in return.

It goes with the saying do unto others as you want them to do to you. When a man feels respected, he will respect you. He'll be able to balance emotions with his natural behavior.

There are a lot of people that just always want things their way. I'm going to be real with you ladies, like I've been from the start. If you feel that everything has to be your way all the time and that what you say goes. You need to destroy this book right away or give it to Shaniqua.

I'm not being funny either, I'm being real. Don't even waste your time with men if you feel as though everything has to be your way because it won't work.

Not because you aren't a good person, not for the fact that you like to yell when you get upset, but because you are not allowing a man to be a man when you feel this way.

If a man doesn't feel like a man subconsciously he will rebel against his oppressor. You would become his oppressor in that kind of relationship.

Trust me when I tell you, you can't abrade your spouse. Webster's dictionary defines abrade as to wear down in spirit or irate. Now to each his own, but I'm going to truly suggest that if you want to get married and stay married, that you not turn your relationship into an abrasive relationship.

If you could add that to your underlined words ladies that would be very helpful. Abrasive

Relationship. The nature of all life is to rebel against oppression.

It might not happen at first but eventually if a man feels as if he cannot be a man in his relationship, he will be forced to rebel against his spouse.

After this comes disloyal behaviors, lying, cheating, or just a loss of interest. This is what a lot of marriages go through, which should not be anyone's goal.

If you really think that you want to be married then you have to try your hardest to play your role as a partner. Never make your spouse feel less of themselves.

Never make your spouse feel like they are in an abrasive relationship. Why? Because he is your help in life. You want your partner to always be strong because if your partner becomes weak in life you become weak in life!

This is a team and only the strong teams can achieve success. Remember when I speak, I'm speaking not just physically. Not just financially but more importantly psychologically.

Love, peace, and happiness is a mental thing. Which cannot be reached if the mind is broken. I know if you haven't been taught about the psychological process of a human, that it might sound hard to learn.

Just keep in mind that your spouse probably hasn't learned about it either. This is what makes this book so powerful because you can start to view life on a psychological level.

You can become in control of your own life! All actions are a reflection of your thoughts. It's a fact that every move that your body makes is a response from what your brain tells it to.

Therefore when you become in control of your thoughts, you become in control of your actions!! Do you want to be a great wife? It starts in the mind.

You have to train yourself to be what you want to be. Yes it will take time, so don't think that you can read this book one time and become someone's wife tomorrow.

The more you think about improving yourself mentally, the better you will become at life. I know you can, you just have to really want to.

Once you want something bad enough you will program your mind to receive it. You can't want something without thinking about it. How can a person say they want a million dollars if they have never thought about a million dollars.

A person knows what they want. The only problem in society is most people don't have the proper education on how to receive what they want. Think about it. Think about it. Think about it!

Everything starts as a thought, then it becomes manifested into action. So let me ask you again.

Why should a woman be submissive to her man?

Lift your head up high and say "I am a queen and I will let my king be a king!"

CHAPTER 5:

Separating the past from the future.

All right now Queen, I got a feeling that you are feeling good within yourself. You know what, I know that you are feeling good within yourself.

First of all you are beautiful, smart, and attempting to take control of your life. You should be proud of yourself for utilizing your brain to achieve happiness.

It's the only way. The only way to better your future is to acknowledge that you are able to take the proper steps to alter any bad behaviors within yourself.

All bad behavior stems from somewhere. Most come from bad thoughts you have and some from certain experiences.

We as people all have to understand that everyone has a past and every one's past wasn't the same. We all have similar situations that have taken place in the past, but for the most part we all have been in different shoes.

Some people forget that their future relationships have nothing to do with their previous ones. Most people learn a lot and take certain behaviors into future relationships.

Sometimes it's good for them, but sometimes this can be bad. A lot of times we hold on to bad things more than good ones. This is bad.

Don't treat your future like it's your past. Unless it worked for you in the past. Did it?

If it didn't work for you then, why would it work for you later? I mean it could, but what are the odds of bad thoughts turning into good actions? Sometimes we try to treat new people the way we were treated or believe that we should have treated the old people. This sometimes can and will hinder you from learning the new person.

You have to treat everyone how they deserve to be treated. You must give your spouse enough respect to say "hey you're not the other guy, so I won't treat you like you're the other guy."

Remember we all have a past, and if you don't want your future to resemble your past. You have to change something. Never look at another person's actions only and judge a relationship.

You should always view your role as well to get the overall view. What role did you play in your past? I mean it is YOUR past.

That means you were there, right?

Then that means you had to participate in it. Now that doesn't mean you were the problem in your previous relationship, so please don't get upset and throw my book.

I'm just saying whatever you did, analyze it and see what you could have done differently. Don't be one-sided to anything because that stops you from seeing the whole picture.

Regardless of what your past relationships were like, your new relationship has nothing to do with it. There's nothing wrong with saying to yourself, " I will never let a man do that to me again."

There will always be key moments in life that alter our view of reality. Just don't let it hurt your future. The new guy didn't do it, so don't treat him like he did.

Give your spouse enough respect to at least give himself a chance to mess up on his own.

Don't hold him accountable for someone else's mistakes. In return, think about what it was in the past that you want to change and lay things on the table for the new guy.

Set new standards, queen, but when you do you have to let this new guy know what these new standards are.

Don't let him be in a relationship where he is blind. This will only hinder you from changing your future. Some women are good at that.

They might have been in a relationship where someone has done something that they didn't let go of. Then when the relationship is over she tells herself never again will she let a man do that same thing.

Never again will she let a man say that and get away with it, but then when she gets a new man she doesn't tell him that she won't allow it.

How would he know what she won't allow unless she tells him. Come on ladies, be real with me because I've been real with you.

How do you expect a man to know what an ex did to you if you didn't tell him. Don't bottle it up and think that he should just know what to do.

It's your responsibility to tell him who you are mentally. No one can read your mind. Give yourself a chance to do something different and be different.

Unless he knows what the difference is, he doesn't understand what you like. This is what is meant when people speak about communication skills.

You and your spouse have to communicate with each other before you get deep into a relationship. That's why I suggest you set standards for your relationship.

How do you want your spouse to speak to you?

How do you want your spouse to respond to you?

How do you want him to treat you?

You can't expect for him to know these kinds of things that you never told him.

Some women assume that men automatically are supposed to know how to treat them. For the most part a man knows that he has to show a woman attention, but that doesn't mean that he will know exactly what kind of attention you need.

Some women like to cuddle at night, while others may want their space.

Some women like to hold hands, while some women feel like she hates when a man's hands are all sweaty.

It's natural for people to have different preferences, but let's just be real. If I had 5 previous girlfriends that love to hold my hand everywhere we go, how would I know that my new girlfriend hates that?

How would I know that her last boyfriend used to squeeze her hand until there wasn't any blood flowing?

I wouldn't know unless she told me. Right?

This is what I mean when I say you have to know how to separate the past from the future. You have to give your future spouse room to be himself and not view him like he is everyone else.

I suggest that you write down your do's and don'ts for your future relationship.

Take your time and think about what was done in your last relationship that made you happy.

What would you want your new spouse to do and what can he do that would make you respect them?

Whatever it is, write it down on the other side of the list. This will get you a better understanding of what type of woman you are and think about what you don't want a man to do to you.

Think about this for a little second because this will stop you from going through the things of the past that are unacceptable for the future.

What did your ex's do to you that would make you look at the next man wrongfully?

What are you not willing to put up with?

Once you finish your do's and don't list then I need for you to study it. I'm not saying read it every second of your life, but what I am saying is read it often.

To be honest with you what I would prefer you do is record it into your phone. Yes I said record the answers on your phone.

As a voice recording.

Now once you are finished, make sure you listen to it a few times a day. If you like to work out, listen to it while you exercise.

I want you to repeat it in your head, what you will and will not accept in a relationship.

I hope you stay true to your word when it is time. Once something is repeated in the mind constantly it becomes embedded into the subconscious mind.

Then your behavior will show improvement. This is first so that you know yourself first and foremost.

Then once you really know where you stand in your mind, you will be ready to teach a man how you want to be treated.

Remember if you don't tell a man what you like, he won't know what you like!

He is just a handsome, smart man, not a mind reader.

When you find the man that you think is a good selection to give attention. Give him a copy of your do's and don't list.

Now come on queen, don't be nervous.

Give him a copy.

In return tell him that you would like for him to write his own about what he feels is acceptable and not acceptable behaviors in a relationship.

Let him know that this is for you two can better understand each other. This will set the law down in your relationship before it gets hot.

This is a great form of communication, because no one has to feel uncomfortable. This is a way to learn what your man likes and doesn't like.

Together, this will help you and your new spouse learn each other mentally.

Remember queen you are aiming for psychological happiness. Knowing your spouse mentally is how you avoid doing things that may harm your relationship.

Now let's just get this out there on the table. I like to cuddle. When I'm feeling good at night and want some bonding time, I want to be close and talk.

What if my next girlfriend was used to dealing with guys that used to yell at her when she tried to cuddle with them. "Move girl, stop," they may have told her.

Imagine what that felt like for her. She probably had that happen to her for years. Now here we are together in a relationship but we don't know each other mentally yet.

We have explained our does and don'ts to each other. We might get in bed together and feel like there isn't a spark between us.

Why because I noticed how far away in the bed she gets from me. I noticed that twhen I tried to cuddle with her the first time and she quickly moved away.

Here I thought she didn't like me in that way. Now we go days without speaking about the situation, so I don't understand why she doesn't seem to enjoy cuddling.

This alone could make me become distant from her mentally because I felt as though I wasn't getting what I want from my new girlfriend.

This one thing could cause problems between us because I have my wants in a relationship, but I'm not getting them. Imagine how much time will go by until this issue is addressed.

A few days, a few weeks, or even a few months. Whatever it is one day we will speak about it, but after so long it might be too late.

I don't want to be in a relationship and I'm not getting what I want. This could have made me value her company less and feel like she isn't for me.

This is why communication plays a big role in relationships. If you don't talk about everything to your spouse they won't know how you feel.

If we would have spoken about our do's and don'ts in the beginning of the relationship, I would have known that she hasn't cuddled with a man in years.

She would have known that I love to cuddle.

If we knew each other psychologically we could have become a great couple. If i would had known from the beginning that my new girlfriend hasn't been getting the love and respect that she deserves from her previous relationships, I could have been the guy that changed that.

Ultimately I could have been the guy that helped her obtain psychological happiness.

I'm saying that this is why I want you to separate the old guy from the future one.

I don't want you to lose out on happiness because you didn't really get to know your spouse psychologically.

Therefore you need to know who you are and vice versa.

Take your time to learn from each other. I promise you it's better to spend the first days, weeks, or months learning about a guy than to have wasted years on a guy that you didn't really know.

This is one of the main reasons why Shanique jumps from relationship to relationship.

Not to make fun of Shanique, but she won't turn a boyfriend into a husband. Shanique doesn't see a problem with not holding deep intellectual conversations with a man.

Do you know what else Shanique does not find a problem with? Go ahead, think about it.

Do you know why Shanique really can't keep a man? Come on now queen I've said it time and time again I'm not going to sugarcoat anything for you.

We're going to be real with each other 100% of the way.

Do you want to know why Shanique can't keep a man?

It's because she doesn't give them enough time to know each other mentally before she gives up the cookie!

Come on man you know what I mean by giving up the cookie.

That good stuff, that wam bam, the oochie wally wally oochie bang bang.

I don't have to spell it out for the kids to hear it.

That's her problem though! She doesn't make any man wait long enough before he gets it, but it's not just her, it's a lot of women.

When I say a lot I mean a lot. Think about it from a man's perspective. If you don't know a female mentally, how can you say you know her?

Quite frankly if you can't say you know her, how could you say you like her?

Of course you know that she is beautiful but you haven't known her long enough to really say that you like her.

One day she gives you some of the good stuff and it was good stuff." Do you know her now?

Do you like now?

Come on, let's be real queen. I'm not being fake with you so don't be fake with me.

Do you like her now?

Of course you don't. You still don't know her.

Good stuff doesn't make people psychologically compatible, but guess what you do like?

Just guess.

In that situation all you know is that you like that good stuff. Now this relationship is not a psychological one, it's a sexual one.

So as a man when you get back around Shanique, you know what you want to get. You want that good stuff, but look what is about to happen.

It always does. No matter if it takes days, weeks, months, or years. You meet someone else. This someone else gives you conversation that catches your attention.

Then you start to want to learn someone else mentally. Why? Because you spent all this time with a woman that you don't know, so think about it.

Of course that good stuff was good, but this new woman is giving you a sense of psychological happiness. Plus on top of that she may or may not have better good stuff.

As a man now, he might take a chance with her because no matter what this new girl seems better.

Why? Once again because love, peace, and happiness is psychological.

So what's your next step if you're in this situation?

Come on let's be with each other, you leave Shanique and go with this new woman.

Hold on we're going to keep it real, so let's keep it all the way real. What happens months later?

I'll tell you. Shanique gets another boyfriend and goes through the same thing in this new relationship. This new one might be a longer one or a shorter one, but she gets the same result.

Look at what her ex is doing with that other woman. She's pregnant. Oh yeah! They're having a baby and thinking about getting married.

Now sorry ladies if that sounds like someone you know. Don't yell at me, I'm not speaking about you, I'm speaking about Shanique.

Now this is the problem with a lot of relationships. Some women, a lot of women, are not giving their spouse enough time to learn them in and out before he gets the good stuff.

I'm not going to give you a time limit on how long you should wait before you give any man you're good stuff.

I'm just going to tell you to make sure you both know and understand each other. What's the rush?

I know queen sometimes you might get the urge, but if this man doesn't deserve it, he doesn't deserve it.

Shanique got the urge and now she's single again. Meanwhile her ex is bonding, cuddling, and starting a family with someone else.

Queen, don't be a Shanique!

Please, I'm not going to ask you if you are or not. I'm not here to judge you. I just want you to elevate things a little. So Queen, rise and separate the past from your future!

CHAPTER 6:

Now it's on you.

Hey queen. You finally made it to chapter 6.

Once again let me say that I am proud of you for taking this seriously. You will definitely not regret this. I can promise you one thing, you did not waste your precious time on me.

Every second counts and now let's get down to the final seconds of my book.

I must be real with you.

Now you know that when I say I'm going to be real with you, I always do. So let's be real.

Before I say it let me just remind you that this is to make you psychologically successful. Don't try to be stuck up now and close the book because it's your turn.

Keep it real with me, queen.

You know what, keep it real with yourself, please.

Are you fit to be someone's wife?

What kind of wife would you be?

Are you worthy of a man getting on his knees and proposing to you?

Do you deserve true love, peace, happiness, and matrimony?

Okay of course you said yes right? If you are so sure, get a sheet of paper and a pen.

Don't play and try to act like you don't have to do this. Are you scared?

Come on I told you I'm going to keep it real with you so I am. If you can't do this for yourself, then maybe you don't have what it takes to turn a boyfriend into a husband.

For all of the beautiful queens that are willing to do whatever it takes to better their future I applaud you and wish you the best in life.

For all of you that are just reading this book because you're bored. Thanks for supporting my book.

Now let's get the paper out.

Are you ready?

Okay let's go then. I want you to write 5 questions down.

1) Why should a man take his time to settle down with you when there are so many other women out there willing to be with him?

2) How can you help a man reach his full potential and become a better man?

3) Can you look a man in the eyes and respect him as your secondary father? How do you know?

4) How would you feel if your man wants you to meet his mother and you see them yell at each other? How would you respond to him?

5) What makes you different from Shanique?

Now ladies please take this seriously because I need you to. This will tell if you are true within yourself.

Be real and answer these questions truthfully because if you don't you're only stopping yourself from gaining true knowledge.

I'm one for searching deep within myself to find true knowledge. If you truly don't understand me you should research the doctrine of self-knowledge.

Know thyself is the motto of the great ancient society of The Egyptians. They explained that self-knowledge is true knowledge.

So with that being said the only way to reach a real understanding of yourself, is to be real when you think about everything. Sometimes we lie to ourselves because we know that our answers for certain questions are not as good as they should be.

Now ladies I'm asking you so many questions, so that you can be real with your answer. Then you can help yourself.

If you read your answers to those questions and it doesn't sound the best to you, that's good. Why? Well because that means that you are truthful and can work to better yourself.

Out of 100 women that take this seriously at least 85 of them will not truly be comfortable with their true answer.

Some of them, excuse me, most of them won't write their first response.

Most just won't really answer these questions to their best ability. Believe it or not. A lot of people can't be 100% honest with themselves because they then would see that they are just portraying to be someone that they are not.

No matter what queen, you are a queen and I want you to know that you have potential to be powerful.

You can be all you can be if you put your mind to it. Just think about it. Everything starts from your thoughts.

Baby girl, how and why should a woman be submissive to her man?

When you are ready to really answer that question, then you are ready to be a better girlfriend than my ex.

A lot of men won't say this, so let me be the first to tell you that I will do anything to become better. This is what makes me different.

I won't let my pride steer me from doing better for myself and my family. I have my own mind and I would never lie to myself.

I wasn't the best boyfriend to my exes and I was a product of my environment. None of my friends treated their women with respect.

None of my friends were good influences.

Now when I think about it, neither was my family, the television, or the music that I put into my ears.

Just like most boys, it took for me to get my heart broken in order for me to sit down and look at my behavior.

I never knew that I was the kind of guy that was a genuine, lovable, smart man until I met the woman that didn't deserve me.

I had two beautiful children from this relationship, which lasted six years. 6 years of horror, brought me to inner peace.

Now I look at my daughter in her eyes. She is the girl that made me change it all.

I can't hurt her.

I would never leave her behind unprotected.

I would give her my last and do whatever it takes to make her happy. This feeling that I have for her is the feeling of true love.

This is why ladies I want you to be real with yourself at all times because there's nothing more satisfying than inner happiness.

Love is a feeling and thought that cannot be hidden. When people really love each other you can tell by the way they look at one another.

You can feel loved when the person that you love looks you in your eyes.

I want every Queen to feel love within her heart and mind.

For every woman this should be your goal when you think about getting into a relationship.

Can you love someone with all your heart? Have you ever sat quietly for hours and suddenly burst into laughter because of your own thoughts?

This is what people do when they are happy. They smile when no one is around to see it!

Do you?

If not, why don't you?

Do you have something to tell yourself everyday that makes you feel good, if you didn't before now you should.

Thank you for reading this book. That shows that you have what it takes to take your relationships in life seriously.

It shows that you want to be happy and I'm going to be real with you Queen. you can.

I know from experience that life can make you feel as if you are missing something that others aren't, but I'll tell you what.

As long as you want peace, love, and happiness the universe will give it to you. Just think about it. Day and night.

Just think about it. Knowledge isn't learned until it is learned.

Information isn't just shared, it's also studied.

Now that you have a little bit more knowledge, it's up to you to take it seriously enough to make it work for you.

It can really work, but only if you let it. Be real with yourself and write down those questions and answer them.

If you're serious about turning a boyfriend into a husband then write your do's and don'ts for a relationship.

If you do have a spouse or someone you're interested in you should put the list on the wall so that you can see it every day.

Continue to think and manifest a wife's attitude. If you display a wife's attitude, you will attract a guy with a husband's attitude. There are plenty of men that will love you, but will you give him the time that it takes to learn who you are?

He won't know if he can love who you are if you don't let him know who you are!

Keep this in mind. Who you think you are, you are!

Will you let a man know who you think you are?

Make sure when you do speak about it is actually true.

You need to really know yourself. Before he can honestly know you, you have to know yourself, you have to know what you like as a whole before getting into a relationship.

Take the time to learn by yourself.

Take yourself on a date. Watch a few movies alone. Take a few walks in the park and talk to yourself.

Don't be afraid to talk to yourself. I do it all the time. It's called thinking out loud.

When you take the time to know thyself you become aware of who you truly are. How can you expect a man to know you if you don't really know yourself?

Peace, love, and happiness comes from within and until you discover love from within, then no one can love you.

I hope you took what I have been saying seriously because I'm going to find out. I want you to post your do's and don'ts list on my Facebook page.

Don't be scared, there is nothing to worry about trust me.

I want you to post it so that I know you took me seriously.

Remember it doesn't hurt me if you don't get married and find true inner happiness. It really doesn't, but I can be honest and say that it would make me feel like I did my part in this world if I knew that I helped other females besides my daughter find true love and happiness. So if you were for real and really want to be happy, post your do's and don't list.

I wish all of you beautiful Queens well in your journey of turning a boyfriend into a husband, good luck queen!!!

Facebook: Neva Eva

Instagram: NevaEvaRecords

About the author;

Hello, I am Isaiah Donaldson Jr the author of this wonderful book.

I am from Newark New Jersey and at this moment in time of actually writing this book I am 27 years old.

I have two beautiful children Amir and Isabella.

I've been through a lot at this time.

I've been incarcerated.

I am not proud to say it, but I am definitely happy to have learned from each and every one of my mistakes.

We as humans do make mistakes and that's one thing that people have to realize.

It is common to make mistakes.

I've been in relationship after relationship after relationship.

So I definitely know a little bit about them.

I'm a great father and for some that may be hard to believe being in the store I'm young and I am African American.

I took my time writing each and every one of my books in the different phases that I was in at the time of writing them.

I never wanted to go on to my next course in life without writing down my previous one.

So after a horrible relationship with my children's mom.

I decided to write this book to inform my future girlfriend how to keep me!
Just because I am from a bad place and have been incarcerated does not mean that I don't deserve to be loved.
It does not mean that I don't know how to treat men.
It does not mean that I am a deadly father.
My past is my past and my future is my future.

I will not use my past as an excuse for my future.
I will use it as a learning tool in order to correct my present, and manifest my future.

Other books by Isaiah Donaldson Jr
- How to raise boy to be a man
- Why we're broke and they're rich
- The first steps to entrepreneurship

- Why boys join gangs

Psalm 37:23, "The steps of a good man are ordered by the Lord: and he delighteth in his way."

Ephesians 5:25: "For husbands, this means love your wives, just as Christ loved the church. He gave up his life for her."

Genesis 2:24: "Therefore a man shall leave his father and his mother and hold fast to his wife, and they shall become one flesh."

Made in the USA
Columbia, SC
18 February 2025

54057913R00069